EXAMINING
VOLCANIC ERUPTIONS

BY JEN MELIN

CLARA
HOUSE
BOOKS

First published in 2015 by Clara House Books, an imprint of
The Oliver Press, Inc.

Copyright © 2015 CBM LLC

Clara House Books
5707 West 36th Street
Minneapolis, MN 55416
USA

Editors: Mirella Miller and Arnold Ringstad
Series Designer: Maggie Villaume

Picture Credits
RZ Design/Shutterstock Images, cover, 1; Shutterstock Images, 4, 10, 16–17, 20, 34; Barry
Sweet/AP Images, 6; U.S. Geological Survey, 8, 27, 28, 33, 36, 38; Dr. Dwayne Meadows,
NOAA/National Marine Fisheries Service/Office of Protected Resources, 12; James Stevenson/
Donks Models/DK Images, 14; National Park Service, 18; NASA, 22; Red Line Editorial, 24;
Lieutenant Elizabeth Crapo/NOAA, 31; Anatoly Gruzevich/VNIRO Russia/NOAA, 40–41;
Karl Briullov, 42

Library of Congress Cataloging-in-Publication Data

Melin, Jen, author.
  Examining volcanic eruptions / Jen Melin.
     pages cm. – (Examining disasters)
  Audience: Grades 7-8.
  Includes an index.
  ISBN 978-1-934545-68-3 (hardcover : alk. paper) – ISBN 978-1-934545-84-3 (ebook)
  1. Volcanic eruptions–Juvenile literature. 2. Volcanoes–Juvenile literature. I. Title.

  QE521.3.M458 2015
  551.21–dc23

                              2014044477

3 1907 00355 0190

Printed in the United States of America
CG1022015

www.oliverpress.com

CONTENTS

ONE

MOUNT SAINT HELENS

Mount Saint Helens in southwestern Washington had not erupted since 1857. But for more than 100 years, the volcano remained active, meaning it could erupt again with little or no warning.

What became a major tragedy at Mount Saint Helens began with a series of small earthquakes on March 16, 1980. A steam eruption followed on March 27. Between March 27 and May 18, there were a series of minor eruptions that occurred in March and April. By May 17, more than 10,000 earthquakes had shaken the volcano. The mountain's cryptodome, or the bulge forming from the buildup of magma and other forces, had grown 450 feet (140 m). The

A quiet Mount Saint Helens sits years after its 1980 eruption.

Authorities asked residents in a 10-mile (16-km) red zone around the volcano to evacuate. But some residents refused to leave despite the danger.

cryptodome's growth was a sign that magma was rising inside Mount Saint Helens and the volcano could soon experience a bigger eruption.

At 8:32 a.m. on May 18, a powerful earthquake triggered a landslide on the mountain's north face. This landslide resulted in the north slope of the mountain falling away, creating an avalanche. It was the largest debris avalanche in recorded history. The avalanche dropped a total of 3.3 billion cubic yards (2.5 billion cubic km) of debris, enough to fill approximately 1 million Olympic-size swimming pools. A lateral blast from the side of the mountain followed the avalanche, spewing a cloud of stone that stretched 17 miles (27 km) into the air. The cloud reached temperatures of 660 degrees Fahrenheit (350°C) and moved at speeds of more than 300 miles (500 km) per hour. The force of the blast knocked down trees.

SURVIVING THE BLAST

Bruce Nelson was fishing on the Green River with friends approximately 13 miles (21 km) north of Mount Saint Helens when the volcano blew. Nelson and his girlfriend, Sue Ruff, fell into a hole where an uprooted tree had been. Being below ground level protected Nelson and Ruff from the worst of the blast, but the heat burned off the hair on their arms. After the blast passed, they hiked 20 miles (32 km) over 12 hours through knee-high ash until rescuers found them. They breathed through their sweatshirts to filter out the ash. Approximately 125 people managed to survive in the blast zone.

A cloud of stone, ash, and dust fills the sky after Mount Saint Helens erupted.

Mud and pyroclastic flows, a mixture of rocks and toxic gases, soon followed the lateral blast.

At the same time as the lateral blast, a vertical eruption took place. This type of event is also known as a Plinian eruption. It is named after Pliny the Younger, who witnessed the eruption of a volcano in 79 CE and recorded his observations. A cloud of gas and ash 16 miles (26 km) high was released. That is more than 58 times the height of the Empire State Building. The cloud dropped ash as far away as Montana. It also covered in complete darkness the city of Spokane, Washington, 250 miles (400 km) away. The Plinian eruption lasted for nine hours. Winds carried 520 million tons (470 million metric tons) of ash across the United States.

AFTERMATH OF THE ERUPTION

The eruption was so strong it changed the shape of the mountain. The old cone-shaped mountain peak was now a crater. The mountain was also 1,314 feet (401 m) shorter than before the eruption.

The eruption killed 57 people and thousands of animals in one of the worst volcanic eruptions in North American history. People died in the

ERUPTIONS SINCE 1980

Mount Saint Helens has erupted many times since 1980, though these eruptions have been much smaller. Between October 1980 and October 1986, 17 eruptions created a new dome of lava that hardened and solidified 876 feet (267 m) above the base of the crater.

The 1980 eruption changed the landscape of Mount Saint Helens, killing plants and trees in its path.

blast of fire and ash or in the mudslides that followed. The eruption caused approximately $3 billion in damages.

MONITORING VOLCANOES

The eruption of Mount Saint Helens was a reminder of the deadly power of volcanoes. These powerful forces of nature can erupt with little or no warning. Because of the disaster in 1980, Mount Saint Helens is among the best-known volcanoes in history. After the eruption, the U.S. Congress funded volcanologists at the U.S. Geological Survey Cascades Volcano Observatory to monitor nearby mountains. Additional observatories were established near other clusters of active volcanoes in the United States. Volcanologists hope that by studying and monitoring volcanoes they can prevent another tragedy like the one caused by the 1980 eruption of Mount Saint Helens.

HOW SCIENCE WORKS
KNOWING SIGNS, SAVING LIVES

If a volcano is changing in shape, it could be a sign that magma and gas are rising. Earthquakes near the site of a volcano indicate movement is occurring underground. Volcanic gases rising from a vent can also mean an eruption will occur soon. These signs are common to many kinds of volcanoes. No matter where the volcano is on Earth, scientists use similar evidence to predict upcoming eruptions.

In 1991, scientists were able to use this type of information to predict the eruption of Mount Pinatubo in the Philippines. Scientists recognized key signs before Pinatubo erupted, giving thousands of people time to evacuate. Because of their work, at least 5,000 lives and $250 million in property were saved.

TWO

THE MAKING OF A VOLCANO

Volcanoes are among the most destructive natural forces in the solar system. They are found not only on Earth, but also on other planets and their moons. On Earth, explosive eruptions have killed more than 200,000 people in the last 500 years. Scientists have counted a total of approximately 1,300 volcanoes on the planet. Most have erupted many times throughout history.

The lithosphere is the surface layer of Earth. It contains the crust and the upper part of the mantle. Earth's lithosphere is broken up into pieces called tectonic plates. The plates slowly slide on the mantle's magma. Most of the world's volcanoes are located where tectonic

About 1,500 volcanoes on Earth are still active.

13

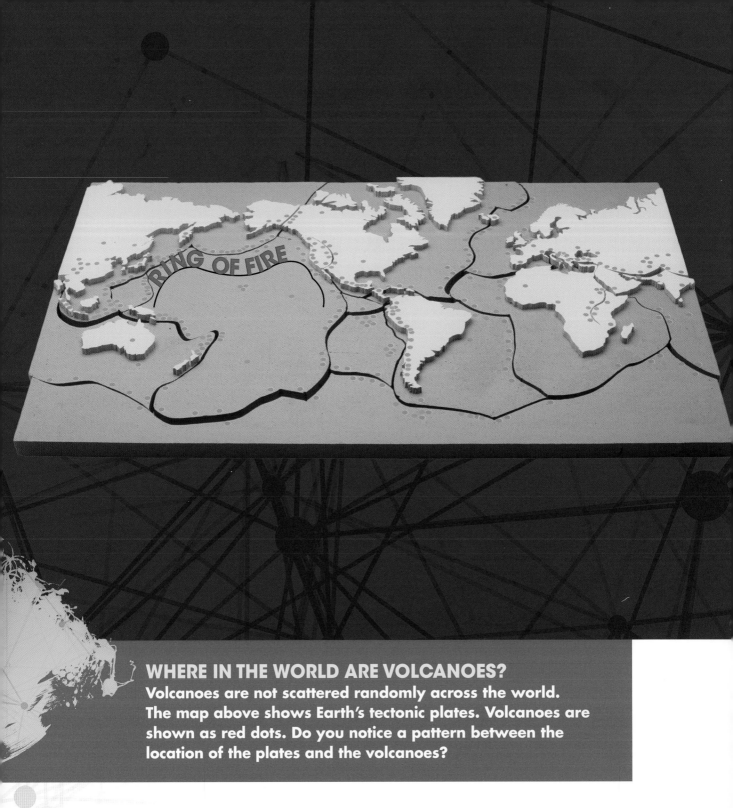

RING OF FIRE

WHERE IN THE WORLD ARE VOLCANOES?
Volcanoes are not scattered randomly across the world. The map above shows Earth's tectonic plates. Volcanoes are shown as red dots. Do you notice a pattern between the location of the plates and the volcanoes?

plates meet and magma breaks through to the surface. Some volcanoes are on land, and others are deep under the sea. Approximately 75 percent of the world's volcanoes are located in the Ring of Fire, a series of tectonic plate borders along the edges of the Pacific Ocean.

When two tectonic plates meet, they can pull apart, push together, or pass by each other. Volcanoes rarely form when plates simply pass by each other. But if plates pull apart, they create a rift between them. The rift fills with hot magma rising up from the upper mantle. The magma cools quickly, forming a new ridge. These formations are called rift volcanoes, and they rarely rise above sea level. The East African Rift System contains many rift volcanoes.

SUBDUCTION ZONES

If tectonic plates meet, the edge of one plate is pushed under the other. These areas are called subduction zones. The plate heats up as it is pushed downward. The heat then pushes magma up toward the surface. On the way to the surface,

A VOLCANO IS BORN

In 1943, a farmer was working in his fields in Mexico when suddenly the ground began to rise. It exploded with ash, vapors, and lava, creating a cone. By the next day, the cone was already about 164 feet (50 m) high. The volcano, known as Paricutin, now stands 1,350 feet (410 m) high. It has given scientists a unique opportunity to study a volcano from its formation.

Mount Rainier in Washington is one well-known subduction volcano.

the magma melts minerals rich with a chemical compound called silica. The silica makes the magma thick and sticky. When the magma erupts through the surface, it is

too thick to flow very far, and it sticks to the sides of the volcano. Over time this forms a tall, steep cone shape.

Nearly all volcanoes form between tectonic plates, but in rare cases they can form in the center of a tectonic plate. Heat can rise from deep inside Earth and melt the

Old Faithful Geyser at Yellowstone National Park erupts approximately every 91 minutes.

rock in the crust. In these hot spots, newly formed magma rises up through cracks in the plate and erupts, forming volcanoes. As the plate slowly moves, the volcano moves along with it, leaving behind islands. The result is a chain of volcanoes, such as the Hawaiian Islands.

HOT SPRINGS AND GEYSERS

If you have ever relaxed in a hot spring or watched a geyser burst, you have seen geothermal activity in action. Magma and hardened volcanic rock near the surface heat the groundwater that feeds the springs and geysers. Yellowstone National Park, famous for its geysers and hot springs, is a hotbed of geothermal activity. The park sits on top of a massive crater left behind from a volcanic eruption approximately 600,000 years ago.

HOW SCIENCE WORKS
NEW EVIDENCE FOR AN OLD THEORY

Most scientists accept the theory of moving tectonic plates under Earth's surface. In science, a theory is much more than a guess. Very strong evidence is needed to call something a theory. By studying volcanoes with modern instruments, scientists have found evidence to support the theory of plate tectonics.

The original ideas about plate tectonics were based on the shapes of the edges of the continents. On a globe, the continents look as though they could be separated pieces of a puzzle. Newer evidence backs up this theory called Pangaea. Scientists have observed that volcanoes and earthquakes happen mainly at the boundaries of the plates. This is where one would expect to find these things if the theory of Pangaea is correct.

THREE

TYPES OF VOLCANOES AND ERUPTIONS

Some volcanoes have such small eruptions that tourists can watch them from just a few feet away. Others are so violent they destroy entire cities. Yet, all volcanoes have some things in common.

Beneath Earth's crust is the mantle, filled with molten rock and gas. Magma from below flows and collects under the mantle until the heat and pressure become too great. The magma chamber cannot contain it any longer, so the magma rushes up a central vent to Earth's surface. It oozes, gushes, or explodes out of the summit crater.

Hikers in Hawaii Volcanoes National Park can get close to active volcanoes.

The Hawaiian Islands are a chain of shield volcanoes.

CINDER CONE VOLCANO

The simplest type of volcano is the cinder cone volcano. Ash explodes from a single vent at the top and falls around the vent in particles and clumps called cinders. The cinders harden, giving the volcano a cone shape with steep sides. Parícutin in Mexico is an example of a cinder cone volcano.

SHIELD VOLCANO

A shield volcano is formed almost entirely by flowing lava. Lava emerges from the summit vent or a group of vents and continues to pour out for a long period of time, flowing down the side of the volcano in all directions. This creates a tall, broad, sloping cone. The final shape looks like a warrior's shield lying flat on the ground.

STRATOVOLCANOES

The deadliest volcanoes are stratovolcanoes. They are made of alternating layers of volcanic ash, lava flows, and cinders. The layers build up to create a tall, steep volcano. Vesuvius in Italy, Mount Fuji in Japan, and Mount Saint Helens are all stratovolcanoes.

CINDER CONE

SHIELD

STRATOVOLCANO

VOLCANO VARIETY
These are images of each of the three volcano types discussed in this chapter. What key differences do you notice? How might these differences give each type of volcano its shape and structure?

SUPERVOLCANOES

Although they form in the same ways as smaller volcanoes, supervolcanoes have stronger eruptions. Their ejecta—ash, lava, rock, and other material that is expelled during an eruption—measures more than 240 cubic miles (1,000 cubic km). The Mount Saint Helens eruption of 1980 spewed 0.06 cubic miles (0.25 cubic km) of ejecta. This is compared to the Toba supervolcano in Indonesia that expelled 770 cubic miles (2,800 cubic km) of ejecta approximately 74,000 years ago. Toba was the largest volcanic eruption in the last 2 million years. Supervolcanic eruptions are so disruptive they can cause changes to the climate. The Toba eruption may have caused an ice age and led to the extinction of many animal and plant species. But supervolcanic eruptions are much rarer than smaller eruptions. The most recent supervolcanic eruption occurred 27,000 years ago in New Zealand.

TYPES OF ERUPTIONS

It is important to know what kind of eruption a particular volcano will produce. Scientists can help keep people safe with this knowledge. Some types of eruptions may have more widespread impacts, requiring a larger evacuation. Different kinds of eruptions are grouped into categories based on their characteristics, but all eruptions can be classified as either effusive or explosive.

In effusive eruptions, lava rises to the surface in flows or fountains. It can also seep through cracks and form huge pools. When the lava cools, it hardens and fills in the cracks. The slow speed of effusive eruptions allows people to escape their paths and as a result, they rarely kill people.

Explosive eruptions, however, produce many hazards because of their suddenness and speed. They can cause

A THIRTY-YEAR ERUPTION

The name of the Hawaiian volcano Kilauea comes from a Hawaiian word meaning "much spreading." The volcano lives up to its name. Since 1983, Kilauea has been erupting slowly and steadily. Over time, it has destroyed small towns and added nearly 1 square mile (2.6 sq. km) of land to the island.

**Poisonous gases, rock fragments, and volcanic ash can kill
people and animals.**

destruction and death on a massive scale. If people do
survive, they are often forced to leave their ruined land,
homes, and cities.

FOUR

VIOLENT VOLCANOES

Volcanic eruptions can cause dramatic changes to Earth's landscape and climate. Even in places far from the eruption, volcanoes can affect crops, transportation, power supplies, and other parts of everyday life.

Volcanic ash is one of the farthest-reaching hazards of an eruption. During a violent eruption, escaping gas rips through solid rock and magma, blasting them into the air. As these materials cool, they form ash. Winds can carry the ash hundreds or even thousands of miles. The ash makes the sky so dark people can hardly see where they are going. Heavy ashfall can cause roofs to collapse. Rain turns ash-covered roads and highways

The first series of eruptions from Eyjafjallajökull in Iceland lasted three weeks.

into slippery mud. Ash clogs and damages cars, roads, and water systems.

LAVA FLOWS

As ash fills the sky, lava flows pour from the vent. The flows move down the sides of the volcano, covering and igniting everything in their way. The speed of a flow depends on the type of lava, the steepness of the ground, and how quickly the lava is coming out of the vent.

Some lava flows move as a wide mass, while others travel through a narrow channel. Because the flows move relatively slowly, people usually have time to escape if there is some warning. The land that the flow covers becomes hardened rock, destroying homes, buildings, and farmland.

GASES

During eruptions, gases in the magma are released into the atmosphere. These gases rise, and

ASH AND AIRPLANES

In April 2010, the Eyjafjallajökull volcano in Iceland erupted. The eruption sent a massive cloud of ash into the air, and the wind carried it toward Europe. People soon realized the ash could jam up jet engines, causing passenger planes to crash. Authorities shut down air travel in northern Europe for more than a week, canceling several thousand flights.

As lava hardens into rock, it ruins everything in its path.

the wind spreads them hundreds of miles. Many different gases are produced, including sulfur dioxide, carbon dioxide, and hydrogen fluoride. Sulfur dioxide can cause

VOLCANIC WINTER

Some massive eruptions expel enough ash and other ejecta to change climate conditions. A large amount of volcanic ash high in the atmosphere reflects sunlight and absorbs heat from the planet below, cooling the planet. The cold conditions, called a volcanic winter, can cause crops to fail, weather patterns to change, and people, plants, and animals to die. In 1815, a powerful eruption came from Mount Tambora in Indonesia. It reduced the average global temperature the next year by nearly 5.4 degrees Fahrenheit (3°C). Therefore, 1816 was called the "year without a summer" in some parts of the world.

acid rain and air pollution. Carbon dioxide is heavier than air, so it collects in low-lying areas. If too much carbon dioxide collects in one place, it can kill people and animals. Hydrogen fluoride in the ash coats plants and poisons the animals that eat them.

LANDSLIDES AND LAHARS

Landslides pose another danger. They can be narrow or broad, ranging from less than 3 feet (0.9 m) across to more than 300 feet (91 m) across. Rock and other debris move down the side of the volcano with so much force the landslide can even cross a valley and run up the side of another mountain. Landslides usually destroy everything in their paths.

If rain or other water is mixed in with the landslide, it is likely a

Lahars can crush buildings, roads, and bridges, and their rocks and debris can bury anything left behind.

lahar will develop. A mixture of water, rocks, and debris, lahars resemble masses of wet concrete rushing down the side of a volcano. Lahars vary in size and shape,

Archaeologists created plaster mummies of people killed when the volcano destroyed Pompeii.

carrying everything from muddy clay to huge boulders. They put people in great danger, because they usually move too fast for people to outrun.

PYROCLASTIC FLOW

The most deadly of the volcanic hazards is the pyroclastic flow. Hot gas and rock blast down the side of the volcano at speeds often greater than 50 miles (80 km) per hour. Temperatures in the flow can reach more than 1,000 degrees Fahrenheit (540°C). Pyroclastic flows bury, shatter, and burn almost everything in their way.

HOW SCIENCE WORKS
PEOPLE OF POMPEII

Buried quickly under ash and rock, the ancient Roman city of Pompeii was well preserved after a volcanic eruption in 79 CE. It was rediscovered and excavated in the 1700s. The victims had long since decomposed, but their bodies left behind empty spaces in the hardened ash. By pouring plaster into these spaces, archaeologists have been able to create casts of the victims in their last moments.

Scientists learned a great deal from these mummies. The molds also filled in the shapes of clothes and household items so scientists could learn about what the people of Pompeii wore and how they lived. The preserved city had paintings, ceramics, jewelry, and religious icons, all of which contributed to a fuller picture of what life was like in Pompeii before the eruption.

FIVE

SCIENCE SAVES LIVES

We still have more to learn about volcanoes. Scientists are working hard to find out more about how to predict eruptions. Volcanologists study the ways volcanoes erupt by collecting and analyzing samples of toxic gases and lava. Geochemists study the rocks, gas, and lava that result from eruptions. Geophysicists study earthquakes to help monitor volcanic activity.

Using sophisticated tools, these scientists try to predict future eruptions. They know an increase in earthquakes often precedes an eruption. They use devices called tiltmeters to detect even the

A scientist collects a gas sample from a volcano in Alaska.

Scientists constantly monitor data to understand volcanic activity better.

slightest change in the shape of a volcano, because a bulge in a volcano can mean magma is rising.

Some scientists specialize in using satellites and cameras to sense volcanic hazards from far away.

Thermal imaging cameras carried by airplanes or satellites take pictures of the heat coming from volcanoes. These images can determine the age of lava flows. Radar mappers create three-dimensional maps of Earth's surface, which help scientists predict the direction of lava flows or landslides.

VOLCANIC EXPLOSIVITY INDEX

Since the 1980s, scientists have used the Volcanic Explosivity Index (VEI) to describe the size of explosive volcanic eruptions on a scale of 0 to 8. To determine an eruption's number, scientists consider factors such as ashfall, pyroclastic flows, the height of the eruption column, and how many hours the eruption lasts. Mount Saint Helens was given a VEI of 5.

BENEFITS OF VOLCANOES

Volcanic eruptions can be devastating, but volcanoes and their eruptions are also beneficial. Volcanic

ENTERING A VOLCANO

Scientists and adventure seekers alike have entered the craters of active volcanoes, either to study them or for the excitement. Temperatures inside active volcanoes are so high that explorers need to wear aluminum heat suits to protect themselves. They also wear gas masks to avoid breathing toxic vapors.

Scientists continue to learn more about volcanoes each year.

deposits eventually break down and become some of the most fertile soil on Earth. Volcanoes rising from the ocean can become islands, and lava flows create new land.

Hot springs, health spas, and mud baths draw visitors to volcanic sites.

Volcanoes are fierce, powerful, terrifying forces of nature that can destroy life and land. Although there is still much to learn, scientists have proved that studying

The people of Pompeii did not know how much damage a volcano could cause.

volcanoes is the first step in predicting where, when, and how they will erupt. As they improve their predictions, volcanologists will be able to save more lives.

CASE STUDY

VESUVIUS

August 20 of the year 79 CE began as a typical day in the ancient Roman city of Pompeii. People bustled about the marketplace, buying and selling goods. The ground began to shake, but the trembling did not worry the people of Pompeii. They did not realize these earthquakes were signs of something much worse to come.

In the afternoon of August 24, smoke billowed up from Vesuvius, a mountain peak about 10 miles (16 km) away. Suddenly, the mountain exploded. A column of volcanic ash reached many miles high and turned the sky black.

That night, the first pyroclastic flow surged down the side of the mountain facing away from Pompeii. Moving quickly, it covered the seaside resort town of Herculaneum. Two more waves followed. A fourth wave rushed down the mountain toward Pompeii. The heat of the flow instantly killed everything and everyone in the city.

TOP TEN WORST
VOLCANIC ERUPTIONS

1. **TAMBORA, INDONESIA, 1815**

   In the largest eruption ever recorded, Tambora killed at least 10,000 people with lava flows and toxic gases. At least 80,000 more died from starvation, as the volcanic ash blocked out sunlight for months, causing crops to fail.

2. **KRAKATOA, INDONESIA, 1883**

   Krakatoa's enormous eruption caused entire villages to disappear. Approximately 36,000 people lost their lives because of the ash and toxic fumes.

3. **MOUNT PELÉE, MARTINIQUE, 1902**

   Residents of Saint-Pierre on the island of Martinique in the Caribbean Sea had been watching the volcano for several days when it exploded. Approximately 28,000 people died.

4. **MOUNT RUIZ, COLOMBIA, 1985**

   Mount Ruiz killed about 23,000 people in the village of Armero. The eruption occurred at night when many were asleep.

5. VESUVIUS, ITALY, 79

The people of Pompeii were killed and remained buried for centuries under ash and rock. An estimated 16,000 people died. In 1631, Vesuvius erupted again, this time killing approximately 4,000 people.

6. KELUD, JAVA, 1586

This eruption killed about 10,000 people crushed by lahars. It erupted again in 1919, killing 5,000 more.

7. MOUNT UNZEN, JAPAN, 1792

The volcano's largest eruption, together with a related tsunami, killed about 14,500 people. It erupted again in 1991 and killed 43 more, including a group of reporters and scientists.

8. LAKI, ICELAND, 1783

Lasting about eight months, this eruption produced a haze that traveled all the way from Iceland to Syria. Poisonous gases, disease, and starvation caused the deaths of approximately 9,000 people.

9. SANTA MARIA, GUATEMALA, 1902

This 19-day eruption caused ashfalls, disease, and starvation that led to approximately 4,000 deaths.

10. LAMINGTON, NEW GUINEA, 1951

Before it erupted, no one knew the volcano was active. It killed more than 3,000 people with a pyroclastic flow.

GLOSSARY

ACTIVE: A volcano that has erupted at least once in the past 10,000 years.

CRUST: The outer layer of Earth.

CRYPTODOME: A formation of magma that builds up inside the volcano, creating a bulge in the rock.

EJECTA: The ash, lava, rock, and other material that is expelled from a volcano during an eruption.

LAHARS: Mixes of water and rock traveling down the side of a volcano that looks like wet concrete when flowing.

LATERAL BLAST: An eruption from the side of a volcano.

MAGMA: Hot, melted rock found below Earth's surface.

MAGMA CHAMBER: An area of liquid rock underground.

MANTLE: The layer of Earth between the crust and the core.

PYROCLASTIC FLOWS: Fluid mixtures of hot, dry rock fragments and toxic gases traveling at great speeds.

RIFT: An opening made by splitting or separation.

SUBDUCTION ZONES: Places where tectonic plates move underneath each other.

SUMMIT CRATER: The top of a volcano.

VOLCANOLOGISTS: Scientists who study volcanoes.

FURTHER INFORMATION

BOOKS

Furgang, Kathy. *Everything Volcanoes and Earthquakes.* Washington, DC: National Geographic, 2013.

Rusch, Elizabeth. *Eruption! Volcanoes and the Science of Saving Lives.* Boston: Houghton Mifflin Harcourt, 2013.

Van Rose, Susanna. *Volcanoes and Earthquakes.* New York: DK, 2008.

WEBSITES

http://kids.discovery.com/games/build-play/volcano-explorer
On this website, users can build their own volcanoes and see what happens when they erupt.

http://video.nationalgeographic.com/video/kids/forces-of-nature-kids/volcanoes-101-kids
This website features a video to introduce readers to volcanoes.

INDEX